HOW JULIA FOUND HAPPINESS AND FINANCIAL SUCCESS

YOUR GUIDE TO MAKING MONEY IN A SERVICE BUSINESS

BY

MICHAEL G. COLBURN

Also by Michael G. Colburn

Invent, Innovate & Prosper

The Inventor's Workbook

Financial Success Guide – Time Based Businesses

PRAISE FOR
INVENT, INNOVATE & PROSPER

...Colburn is extremely thorough in covering the steps necessary to be a successful inventor. Highly recommended.

Crystal R.

...guides the reader through the innovation process step-by-step with readable language and a sprinkling of humor to keep his book enjoyable while being thoroughly educational.

Carl W.

What is so fantastic about this book is how simple and accessible it is.

Hanna B

Einstein, Tesla, Edison; some of the world's best creative minds and inventors. What did they all have in common? The unique and communicative mindset that Michael Colburn masterfully guides his readers to.

Kite

Invent, Innovate and Prosper is a really useful and inspiring guide.

Katherine P.

The Power in Colburn's approach is how he leads the would-be inventor from a simple idea, to a well-researched product, and beyond to commercialization.
Lauren

...A fantastic book that will teach you everything you need to know to become an inventor.
Ed M.

This was a great book...reading was easy to follow, pacing was great.
Tanya

This book covers the ABCs of inventing. ...well written and goes deep into the main areas that help the inventor through the process to invent a product.
Fred F

...an engrossing read...using real world examples and sharing stories of notable inventors, writing is solid...also can be used as a tool to help jumpstart any creative project.
Rachel

I would recommend this book for any rookie inventor
Ravin M.

...puts reader on a journey to creating their inventiveness.
Mark S.

...creates an easy to understand "roadmap" that will help anyone to solve the problems they have identified...this book will not only help you in many ways, it will also inspire you.
Jon E.

I loved that the book started with mental preparation.
Customer Reader

I was fascinated by the section when Colburn addresses how to intentionally have a cooperative mind functioning...
Al J

...a step by step method for confronting problems and arriving at practical solutions
William K

TABLE OF CONTENTS

INTRODUCTION

In my career of more than five decades as a creative entrepreneur, a design and engineering firm founder, and eventually the founder of Ideas Well Done, a company specializing in inventing where I was surrounded by smart and creative designers and engineers, I made about all the financial mistakes one can make. I learned from my mistakes and moved on to solving them. I thought I could save others a lot of time and aggravation if I could write a small book describing the financial tools for time and service-based business. Having written two non-fiction how-to books in the last couple of years, I decided I wanted to tell a story and not just provide a set of guidelines. This is a work of fiction with a lot of real-life lessons on succeeding financially in a time-based service business.

I hope you find this valuable and entertaining.

If you visit www.inventingpathways.com and add your name to our mailing list, you will be able to download valuable documents for free. We will not abuse or share your email, but occasionally, I may drop you a note to let you know of a new book or useful information you may be interested in.

Thank You!

TIME WISDOM

I bargained with Life for a penny, and Life would pay no more. However, I begged at the evening when I counted my scanty store. For Life is a just employer, he gives you what you ask. But once you have set the wages, why, you must bear the task. I worked for a menial's hire, only to learn, dismayed, that any wage I had asked of Life, Life would have willingly paid.

Jessie Belle Rittenhouse (Rittenhouse, 1939)

———————

Time is Money

Benjamin Franklin

(Franklin, 1748)

———————

I remember to have heard of a notable Woman, who was thoroughly sensible of the intrinsic Value of Time: Her Husband was a Shoemaker, and an excellent Craftsman; but never minded how the Minutes passed. In vain did his Wife inculcate to him, That Time is Money: He had too much Wit to apprehend her; and he cursed the Parish-Clock, every Night; which at last brought him to his Ruin.

Quote from the periodical "The free Thinker" (1719)

———————————

CHAPTER 1

JULIA

2009

Four years ago, at the ripe old age of thirty-seven, Julia was widowed. Carl literally was hit by a bus—stepped right in front of it, just like in the movies. He had just purchased a bouquet for their anniversary and was holding the flowers up so Julia could see them from her third story office. She had not been looking, which she was very thankful for later. Carl had been her high school sweetheart; they'd married at twenty-two. Julia had eleven years of married happiness and then a deep dive into grieving. Now she occasionally found herself smiling at a photograph of some trip they'd taken or remembering one of his deadpan comments, which he really meant to be funny, and sometimes were. They'd never had children, though they'd tried. She occasionally still talked to him in her head and even thanked him for the time they'd had together, she would always cherish it.

Julia was a senior designer for toys and games at Bell Brothers, a company specializing in product development and design for multiple industries. One of the casualties of dealing with the loss of her dearest friend was her job—

she just didn't care about it, wasn't focused on getting anything creative done, creativity seemed to have a blinder on. After a few months of accomplishing very little, she gave her notice and resigned before she disappointed her clients, some of whom had been with her since her first day at work.

She had some savings, a 401K she could dip into if necessary, and Carl had an insurance policy that was not huge but was more than two years of her salary. She leased her condo to Cindy, a girlfriend and her model maker at Bell Brothers who wanted a larger, furnished place, and Julia bought a ticket to Paris. Three weeks in Paris was enough, she wanted a smaller quieter city. She bought a train ticket to Avignon where she rented a second-floor apartment overlooking a small square with a bakery coffee shop, a bar and restaurant, and a candy shop. She shopped at the famous *Halles d'Avignon* market, sipped coffee in one of its cafes, and observed people going about their everyday lives. Returning to her apartment, she prepared simple meals and sat on her balcony watching the locals and the tourists walk by, mostly couples. She learned to communicate in French—barely, but she managed. Occasionally, passers-by would wave and offer a friendly *Bonjour*, she replied with an air toast of her Côtes du Rhône and returned the greeting. She was lonely, missing Carl but was coming to terms with her situation. She didn't want a romantic relationship, but to be honest with herself, she came to the conclusion she missed working, the creative pursuit and interaction with others. Besides, the money would not hold out forever.

"Mr. Bell, Julia Collins here, I'm calling from France."

"Hi, Julia, nice to hear from you, how are you doing?"

"I'm doing well, but I'm bored. I was wondering if you might consider having me come back to work for you"

"You know I think a lot of you, but I'm closing up shop, Julia, I'm over seventy, and its time for me to retire. My nephew Justin is going to take over the appliance design section but will be trimming employees, and, well, quite frankly, the toys and games has not been a big focus for us recently. Sorry, Julia."

They said pleasant good-byes and promised to be in touch when Julia was back in town.

That night, Julia woke from a sound sleep at 4:00 a.m. full of energy. Further sleep was out of the question. She ground some dark roast coffee beans and prepared a French press. She sat at her kitchen table looking out into the dark over her cherished square and began writing a business plan. Accounting for the time difference, she waited for early morning back on the east coast and called Cindy.

"Cindy, Julia from France—I always feel I have to say that don't know why—anyway, do you want a roommate? I can take the small bedroom, but I'll need to use the den to set up an office."

"Hi, Julia, you're way ahead of me! I was going to call you. I may not be able to keep the condo I just lost my job at Bell Brothers."

"I'm sorry, I thought that might happen. I spoke to Mr. Bell earlier, and he filled me in on the changes. Cindy, I am going to start my own firm—do you want a job? Currently without pay, but it includes rent until we are up and running."

Cindy laughed. "Those terms are acceptable for a while; I was going to move back to my parents' basement and live in humiliation. Throw in some food, and we have a deal."

CHAPTER 2

EARLY SUCCESS

Julia and Cindy set about converting the condo into a space they could live in and begin business operations. Luckily, the garage was heated so Cindy could set up a few tools, and Julia purchased two used desks, a bookcase, a file cabinet, and two new computers for the den. She got a new cell phone account for the business and set up new email accounts for her and Cindy.

Julia met with Mark Darden, an old friend who she and Carl knew well who had a very successful business consulting firm which included counseling, accounting, and a business law practice.

"Mark, I can't afford to hire you right now, but I'm starting my own design firm, and I just need to set it up properly to get started. I'm naming it Intriguing Design & Development. We'll design toys and games like we did at Bell Brothers, but will extend into the world of electronic games, home appliances, and devices."

"Julia, don't worry, the first consultations are always free, when you're hugely successful, I'll charge you a bundle."

Mark did a name check and registered an LLC business organization online in less than a half hour. Julia was official.

Cindy and Julia wrote personal letters to every potential business client they knew and many that they didn't know, advising each of their expertise, the services they would be performing, and advising that they would give them a call in the next few days to see if there was a possibility for a meeting. They targeted fifty letters a week, fifty attempted calls each week, with the hopes of five interviews a week. They did arrange some meetings with old clients quickly, others said there weren't any new projects just then but to stay in touch, others told them they were well supported already but would keep the firm in mind.

They landed their first job on a Tuesday of the fourth week of marketing and felt no guilt popping a long-awaited bottle of Champagne—carried from France—at three in the afternoon.

Business grew rapidly, and between the business functions, marketing, meetings, and new interviews, the days disappeared. They worked seven days a week, often into the evening. This went on for nine months, and while both were now paid, they were also exhausted. Julia was shocked at the success and the size of the backlog she had already accumulated—however, she knew marketing could not let up. She had to outsource some electronic designs at a hefty fee on several jobs, but electronic design control was highly profitable. She began looking for an electrical engineer, then a mechanical engineer, a designer to assist her, and the firm grew.

One day, Cindy announced that her father was ill, and she would move back to Cleveland to help care for him. Cindy wished Julia luck, and they hugged. Julia would miss her, but she knew turnover was part of being in business, she began looking for another model maker immediately. When she interviewed a young girl who had just graduated from RISD with no experience but a great personality, and her name was Cindy, how could she not hire her? She gave Cindy1 a nice bonus for all the effort she had contributed to getting started,

As they grew, she couldn't fit the new hires into her condo, so she began searching for a reasonable space to move into. She had a sizeable number of projects which kept growing; customers liked their work and brought more projects back to them, so she only worried about the money a little. She owned her apartment and took a second mortgage to set up a small line of credit to help with cash flow. She found an out-of-business cupcake shop with a kitchen area that would make a nice model shop and an adjacent area that had been a separate storage room. She made an offer to the landlord for both spaces and requested new lights and fresh paint. She maxed out her credit cards for computers, software, desks, some new shop tools, and other necessary operating equipment to accommodate new employees. They moved in twenty-four months from the day she founded the business.

CHAPTER 3

GROWING UP

As Julia sat in Mark's conference room, she felt like a fifth grader sent to talk to the principal for bad behavior. Mark had continued to field a few questions from Julia, which he had never billed, but starting a month ago, Julia had asked if he would take her firm on as a client and help her with finance. Mark's consulting firm was the premier business advisory and accounting firm in the city, and most of his clients were long established firms from all over the region, but Julia felt there was no harm in asking. He jumped at the chance, even giving a "friend and family" discount for services.

Just yesterday, Julia had delivered the accounting records she and a part-time bookkeeper kept to Mark's office, and a day later, Mark had called to ask if Julia could come in and talk with him about the finances. Hence the principal's office gut feeling.

Mark entered carrying a cardboard box with the Amazon swish on the side—the same one in which Julia had delivered the financials on Monday.

"Morning, Jules." Mark liked nicknames, Julia did not.

"Hi, Mark, am I in trouble?"

"Well, let's say we want to keep you out of trouble"

"Oh-oh"

"Jules, you've grown your business impressively over nearly three years in business, but from looking at the box of finances you delivered… do you know the last time I got a box with receipts and accounting notebooks… never mind, it's not important. What is important is that you've grown from working in your spare room to seven highly skilled designers and engineers, and you aren't making a dime more profit than you did when you worked with just one helper."

"Tell me about it," Julia said. "I still use my line of credit on the house to meet payroll half the time. I've paid off significant credit card debt but need new computers, software, and tools now. I knew I needed help, Mark. I didn't really know where to begin."

"The good news is that you seem to increase your work volume every year, your reputation is growing, and clients enjoy working with you. Let's get you profitable. First, a couple of basic fixes immediately, and then I'm going to take you back to the basics of running a time-based business, and we'll get this ship righted."

Julia looked Mark in the eye. "I don't know if I can afford to pay you for the time that will take."

"Jules, you will be able to when we are done, don't worry. First, the quick fixes. I didn't see any client contracts in your material, do you have any?"

"No, I never have. I write a quote and when the client says go, we go."

"OK, I'm going to have an associate pull a couple of samples together from the contracts we use, and then we can discuss what will work for you with one of my junior lawyers. But promise me that from now on, you will review and have executed a real contract with each new job you take. Your clients expect you to do this, and it will protect you in many ways that you might never need, but it is important. Okay?"

"Okay," Julia conceded.

"Now, for me, here is a biggie, and your contracts will help you fix this in the future, but your receivable aging is way out of line. Some are over ninety days, some much longer. Nobody can run a small time-based business without collecting what's owed them in a timely fashion."

Julia squirmed in her chair. "I know. That bothers me, and eventually I call, but most of my clients are repeat, and I hate to make an issue of it."

"Jules, you will go out of business by financing your clients' businesses, and that is what you are doing. When you sign a contract, review the payment terms in detail, let the client know when to expect bills and let them know you need to be paid in a timely fashion or you can't keep working on the project."

"Harsh! "Julia exclaimed.

"Maybe. Everyone who is in business will know this is just business being done well, and it will eventually enhance your reputation as a business owner. When do you bill?" Mark continued.

"Umm," Julia hesitated and squirmed again. "Well, sometimes I'm too busy, so it gets postponed until I get a break, or I'll take the billing home for the weekend and try to get it done then, sometimes that works."

"As I expected," Mark added in a soothing voice. "I did the same thing myself when I first started, but it only makes matters worse. If you do not bill, you do not get paid. When clients do not get bills in a timely fashion, they are more casual about processing and paying them. Fixing your billing and collecting will go a long way toward not having to visit that credit line of yours. For the time being, I suggest, and I suspect this will be hard for you, but take all your overdue receivables and start making calls. Just be honest, you need to be paid in a timelier fashion to keep delivering quality work. Try saying 'is it possible to get paid this week on your overdue bill'—something of that nature. Jules, you love your firm, I know. This is the only way.

When can we get back together and begin a deeper dive into your finances?"

Julia chose the following Monday bright and early.

Back at the office, she printed copies of all outstanding invoices and stacked them in reverse order based on how old each was. She didn't want to make these calls, but she couldn't show up Monday at Mark's without having done so. She was relieved when her project manager Graham asked to talk with her, she could put it off a little longer.

"No one has had a raise in a year, Julia. I know cash is tight but..."

I would rather be making collection calls, Julia thought. She promised to make raises a discussion at the next staff meeting.

Monday morning, 8 a.m. Julia arrived at Ravel and Hayes before Mark did. Veronica, Vern to Mark, the—very perky for 8 a.m.—office assistant to Mark offered Julia coffee. She might have refused since she had two cups already, but Ravel and Hayes had a routine of keeping hazelnut coffee brewed so the smell permeated the waiting area, enticing visitors to indulge themselves.

"Sorry I'm late, Jules, I overslept, I'm getting old, I guess." He was forty-five and she knew he was a very active, youngish forty-five. They went to Mark's office.

"How did the collecting go?" Mark Asked.

"I got about half done and left word for a few others. I got some promises but no checks yet. The first few were hard, but nobody got angry or fired us."

"Of course not! Being paid is part of being in business. Probably some of your clients were embarrassed. but trust me, they understand. I want to make a couple more suggestions on billing and collecting, then we can get serious about operational functions of your business. Here is what I would advise. Hire a bookkeeper with a great phone personality and make it part of the responsibility to make the calls every day. Look at all your accounts to see what can be billed each week, you do not need to wait to the end of the month and bill everyone at once. By doing this, your cash flow will become smoother. Add a billing clause to your contract allowing periodic payments when time has accumulated. Have the bookkeeper call the bookkeeping department of anyone exceeding thirty days—if it goes forty-five days, you call your client."

"Mark, I really can't hire anyone right now, everyone wants a raise, and I have to say no. I can hardly make payroll now. If I hire someone, I could have an uprising."

Mark paused, "Okay, for now, you must do it all yourself. But as the cash improves, I would suggest you get help in this area. You have seven people producing work, yourself included, and only one part time bookkeeper a few hours a month. And you are all probably doing your own office work, which means taking time away from your revenue generation work. You'll need support help eventually to get profitable and cash flow positive."

Julia just nodded. He was right, she just felt she needed to find a way to generate more revenue.

"You're in a time-based creative business, so to start with the basics, we start with time. Your financial success is entirely based on how you measure and monitor time and how you apply what your time records convey to you. What is your time sheet like?"

"We each keep our own time on our computer calendars, and we enter our work for the day at the end of each day, of course, sometimes we forget and fill it in the next day."

"Bingo, no offense, but it's as I thought. I was guilty early on as well. Here is what I learned—you never get it right if you wait until the end of day. You need an official time sheet, a paper one that everyone fills in in fifteen-minute blocks and turns in at the end of every day. I know it sounds excessive, and you will get some pushback, but time is the product your business sells, it's your only resource to achieve financial success. You have to treat it as a precious gem because it is."

"We used to use a time sheet at Bell brothers, it did seem to work well," Julia recalled.

"All your revenue, whether billing the hours or charging them against a fixed fee, is based on the time you and your staff put into projects. Time is your tool to manage employees and projects and profits." Mark reached over onto the blotter of his desk and picked up his time sheet for the day—Veronica had placed it on his desk.

"Here's mine for the day." Vern had entered meetings at appropriate times but there were ten hours of blank hours broken into 4 blocks with a notation line next to each.

Mark continued, "Whenever I complete a task, even if I am going to continue working on the same client, I fill in the block increments and note what the task was. This helps analyze where the time goes, what eats it up, and where the waste is. Time is a very limited resource, you cannot make any more or get any wasted time back. Every employee must do this, it's a cardinal rule here.

"Over here," Mark pointed to the right side of the sheet where there were two check boxes, we note if it's direct time or indirect time, i.e. client time or non-chargeable time."

"We only keep track of project time at the moment," Julia confessed.

"Jules, it's important to track all hours even when they are not revenue hours. We will get into this more in a few steps. I'll ask Vern to give you a copy of this form when we're done."

Vern was more than pleased to give Julia a copy but also said she should have the time instructions from the employee manual and sped off to the file room at double time saying she would be right back.

Usually, Julia held an employee meeting Monday mornings to map out the progress that needed to be made that week on projects, but she'd asked Graham, the project manager, to arrange a lunch meeting instead and to have pizzas brought in.

I'm going to be late for pizza, Julia thought as she drove back to her office, *which means no pizza for me.* Perhaps that would be better, the raise issue was to be a topic of discussion, and she was dreading it.

Julia maintained an open communication policy with employees, so almost nothing was off the table as far as group discussions were concerned. Information that was personal to each employee could not be discussed, but other than that, it was fair game.

There was pizza left, ham and pineapple, her least favorite. Everyone knew it. So, after slipping a piece onto her plate, they pulled out the pepperoni they had set aside. Julia knew the raise issue would come up next, so she started it.

"Look, I know you all deserve raises, and hear me out, I can't afford it, the business can't afford it, but I have started a process of streamlining this operation so that we can make money, give raises, afford new computers, and tools, whatever, perhaps even profit sharing—when we have some—but I can't do this alone. I want to enlist your support in all the steps to make it happen. We have five months until year end, and we will assess raises based on how successful we are in the first quarter after we close out the year."

Tara, an intern, and newest employee asked, "Are you going to share the finances with us?"

Julia hesitated, and then said, "Absolutely. Line by line"

"To get the finances right, I need bookkeeping help, even though that will put further strain on cash, but it will free more of my time for billing, are you all okay with that?"

They understood.

After lunch, Julia called Mark and made a new suggestion. "Mark I don't care what it costs as long as I can have the time to pay it, but I want to make this project of making my business a money machine a company-wide effort and involve all my employees. I want to change our sessions to group sessions here at the office."

"What a great idea," Mark said. Julia was relieved. "I think that's great, in fact, I'm working on a course to give to business students next year, and I can use this as development time. I might even give you a break on the time cost."

"Is that a good lesson?" Julia asked in jest, "and by the way, you already are."

"Because I can," Mark said, "let's make sure you are in my same spot a few years from now."

Julia spent part of the weekend designing a paper time sheet and rewriting employee guidelines on time tracking tailored to her product design business. She emailed them to Mark and Graham. She added a note to Mark in a second email, 'Please call me Julia in front of my employees.' Mark responded, "Of course!!! Jules."

CHAPTER 4

LESSON ONE

TIME TRACKING

Mark arrived early, 7:45, before Julia at 7:55, and Julia was surprised. He was sitting in his car in front of Julia's facility. "I'm just excited about this," he said. "This is new for me, doing the same thing every day can be boring after all these years."

Everyone gathered in the conference room. Graham knew Mark, and other employees had seen him visit a couple of times to take Julia to lunch. Not knowing who he was but suspecting some romantic connection made speculating fun for them, but Julia did a formal introduction, touting Mark's success and expertise and emphasizing that Mark had agreed to be their coach as they converted this busy business into a prosperous entity.

Everyone cheered at this last line.

Mark spent the next hour emphasizing the importance of time and recreating the discussions that he and Julia had at their initial meetings. He reinforced the need for bookkeeping, billing, and collecting help.

"I understand that this is now a team effort and we're—and I am including myself—in a crusade to turn this busy consulting and design practice into a money-making machine. Is that correct?"

Everyone agreed enthusiastically.

"Let's start with time keeping." Groans erupted, eventually followed by smiles.

Mark fired up his laptop and cast a picture of the new timesheet to the screen and proceeded to explain the importance of tracking indirect non-charge time as well as charge or billing time. "And you will note these are daily time sheets, to be turned in at the end of every day."

Mark continued, "All time that isn't billed or charged against a fee to a client is indirect time, it includes vacations, sick days, meetings that are not client related, trade shows. It includes any time spent marketing which is tracked in its own category. It's a ratio that's important, and you all will get better at time management by tracking all your work time."

Adele, an electrical engineer asked, "Why is it important to turn a sheet in every day?"

"It's a fair question," Mark replied. "Many firms gather time sheets at the end of the work week. The importance to turn them in daily right now is for Jules, oops, I mean Julia," everyone sniggered, except Julia. "It's important for her to get a better understanding of the work performed daily, and it will help her measure efficiency, and forecast revenue. It also helps all of you develop the habit of detailed regular time monitoring and seeing how you are performing against your time goals. We have not discussed time goals yet, but we will. After a while, you might want to go weekly or more likely to a cloud program that will track and formulate data on your time usage. But I am old school, and our firm is still on daily paper reports.

CHAPTER 5

LESSON TWO

CHARGEABILITY

"I'll say it again, you are in a time-based business—your salaries and benefits and future raises are based on how much time you spend generating time-based revenue. What would you estimate as the percentage of all your combined time that generates billing or is charged toward project fees?" Each employee and Julia had a piece of paper to write a number on as a percentage. For the seven of them, it ranged from fifty to seventy-five percent.

"Julia, you have the benefit of last weeks' time sheets, what was the total?"

"forty-five percent," Julia answered. "Which included one eight-hour sick day, and we took a trip as a group to the home show at the convention center Tuesday afternoon—all indirect time."

"Fine," Mark said "it's a one-week snapshot. Every week will be different. Every firm over time creates a revenue ratio made up of the cumulative billing percentages of all employees. By the way, we count not just production employees but office staff, administration—everyone, as you add some of these positions. Here, I'll show you how this is calculated."

He drew a simple chart on the white board

	Marketing Hours	Direct Hours	Indirect Hours	Total Hours
Employee 1	0	25	15	40
Employee 2	0	35	05	40
Julia	10	30	20	60
Bookkeeper			10	10
Total	10	0	50	150

"I made this up, but, if we take this as a total firm for one week, we have a total of 150 working hours and ninety direct or billing hours. Ninety divided by 150 equals a sixty percent revenue generating ratio, or some call this the FIRM CHARGABILITY ratio. That's not bad or great but what does it mean? It means that sixty percent of all company time must pay all salaries and expenses of the firm. My estimate is that most time billing firms range between fifty percent and seventy-five percent revenue efficient, the fifty percenters are underperforming and perhaps losing money, and the eighty percenters are doing fine on revenue but might need more support staff to effectively control and maintain efficient business operations."

Randy, a mechanical engineer asked, "So, for the new bookkeeper, and anyone else we add, all of us have to produce more billing hours, we'll burn out at some point."

Mark paused and said, "It's natural to feel that the burden falls on you to produce more, but there is much more to having an efficient profit-generating operation, so I just ask you to work with me until we take a few more steps. We'll get into individual performance next.

"Sure," Randy replied.

"So, let's get into the next step of making this time tool work to bolster the success of this firm."

Everyone nodded.

"You all need to have personal direct time goals that you must monitor in order for the total firm to hit its revenue chargeability goal." No nodding, a couple of groans.

"These will be personal chargeability goals. Understand, you have them now, you just don't know what they are, but they are reflected in your financial statements. If you each know when you are carrying your percentage of the load, you will all benefit."

No rebellion occurred, so Mark continued. "Your responsibilities are all different, and your disciplines are different, and your job expectations are different, so each person's direct time goal will be slightly different than most others. Julia, as the firm grows and you must spend more time in administrative duties, marketing and so forth, it is natural that your revenue ratio will decline. Many principals in mature firms bill at fifty to sixty percent where you are probably around eighty percent by working a lot of extra hours, is that fair?"

"Fair," Julia said.

Graham asked, "My time is split between direct job work and supervising projects as well as general firm duties, like pizza buying," he glanced at Julia, she curled her lip at him, teasing. "How would I set a direct time goal when it varies all the time?"

"Graham, there are some industry standards, but I think you and Julia, with a few weeks' time sheets, can adjust your goal to what is reasonable. I don't know how you track your time at the moment, but remember that if your supervision duties directly relate to a project, then it is direct time, if it's unrelated to a project it isn't, I've seen supervisors who didn't track their supervising time because they considered it management. Use your judgement, but I suspect much of your supervision is a client-based activity."

"True," Graham said.

"Julia, before our next session, will you take a stab at setting direct revenue goals for each employee? This would be a percentage of their hours as chargeable, and by the way, I am traveling next Monday, perhaps we can make it another day or skip a week."

"It's going to be a busy week, Mark, with a couple of deadlines looming, let's just skip."

"Good," Mark replied. "The advice I would offer is to set the goals, taking into consideration each person's indirect expectations. You mentioned a trade show you all attended, that would be indirect, of course."

Julia waited for the end of the following week and took three weeks of full-time records home with her for the weekend before the next lesson session.

She started with herself. Mark had cautioned her not to treat her time differently than others just because she was going to continue to work overtime, skip holidays and vacations some time. He said it would skew the benefits of tracking time. She should use standard work hours and breaks for herself. The extra time was to be tracked in real life but not to be counted on for goal setting.

So, she wrote on a yellow pad,

ME   40 hrs. Week x 52 weeks = 2080 Annual Hours
       Less

           Vacation 80 hours

           Holidays 80 hours

           Sick Days (R&R days) 40 hours

           =1880 hours

           Less

           Marketing 10 hours week (50 weeks) 500 hours

           Administration 2 hours a day, 5 days week,
           50 weeks = 500 hours

I'll consider the trade shows as part of admin, she thought.

She was shocked—if indeed she followed this work plan, it left 880 hours in the year or just about 18 hours a week to bill an acceptable amount of revenue. Running a revenue percentage, she calculated (880/2080 = 42%). She knew she would be doing more at least in the near term, but this just was not adequate. A productive principal, Mark had said would have to be at least fifty percent.

Some of the less-involved marketing activities, like lunch at the Chamber of Commerce monthly meeting could be passed to Graham or Cindy. She had thought for a while that Cindy's personality could win over a few clients, and she would love it. Julia decided to delegate some of the marketing and cut to 8 hours a week on her time budget or (8X50 = 400 hours). She decided to focus administration by delegating some more to Graham. Their firm meetings were very unstructured, although she felt them important—if they set a reasonable time structure and had an agenda, she could save everyone some time. She decided to trim administration time to 350 hours, if it didn't work, she would just skip getting sick or something. The new calculation was now:

1880 hours, less Marketing 400 hours, less Administration 350 hours = 1130 hours.

(1130/2080 = 54%) It was a good percentage. It would have to do for now.

Since she was changing some of Graham and Cindy's time, she would do them next.

Graham filtered down on the top line to the same 1880 hours.

Much of his job management was revenue time but not all, and Julia was increasing his administration duties a little.

She allowed the 250 hours to Graham for indirect administration time, thinking this might be high but she could monitor it with the time sheets. He occasionally participated in client pitches, perhaps two hours a month, say twenty-four hours, and wrote proposals, calculated budgets for the proposals, say four hours a month, forty-eight hours. Got pizza—too bad Julia paid, he ate. This sifted down to 1880-250-24-48 =1558 revenue hours; 1558/2080 = 75% revenue goal.

Cindy worked every day making models or prototypes of designs for the designers, a good eight hours of revenue time. She occasionally found herself waiting for designs to keep up with her pace, however. If Julia started bringing her along in marketing, it might be minimal time to start, but Julia decided to allocate three hours a week to make up for her cutback and some training in marketing time, so, 3x50 =150 hours. Since she had started as a trainee right out of school, Cindy was still at one weeks' vacation, which would change at the end of the year, but they would revisit all revenue goals after year end anyway. So, starting at

1920 hours, less 150 hours = 1770 hours. She was required to attend some design meetings as training, not project time hours and occasional trainings with vendors but not often, say fifty hours a year (1770-50 = 1720 revenue hours = 1720/1920 = 89.5% say 90%).

When the exercise was done, Julia took her laptop and created the chargeability target document for Monday's meeting, and emailed it to Mark and Graham.

Julia considered the weekly staff meeting and decided it would have to be part of indirect percentages for everyone, and everyone was going to put in a little extra time anyway, as they did now. They were not strict time clock punchers. These percentages were to be minimum requirements.

Chargeability Targets (Balance of the year)

Julia-Principal	54%
Graham - Project Manager	75%
Cindy - Model Maker, part time Marketing	90%
(note changes when vacation increased to two weeks)	
Adele - Electrical Engineer	85%
Randy – Mechanical Engineer	85%
Clark – Designer	85%
Tara – Intern	90%

Before Julia could put the laptop away, Mark emailed. "Can you find time to calculate a number for our meeting Monday and email it to me before the meeting?"

Julia replied she would, "What do you need?"

"Please calculate the salary costs for time charged to projects—just the bare costs, not the benefits or taxes or anything, just the time based on each salary and the percentage of chargeability targets you sent me."

Hmmm! Julia thought, we are just getting started, I think. But she did feel for the first time that she was getting a handle on the management of her business. She sat back down at the desk and went to work.

Salaries

ME	$130,000	54%	$70,200
Graham	80,000	75%	64,000
Cindy	48,000	90%	43,200
Adele	70,000	85%	59,500
Randy	65,000	85%	55,250
Clark	55,000	85%	46,750
Tara	37,000	90%	33,300
Total	$485,000		$380,746. (381,000)

Julia emailed the spreadsheet to Mark.

Mark wrote back—Julia was ready for dinner now—and asked if salaries were known among employees.

"Yes, we're completely open with everything at work," Julia replied, adding. "now I'm going to eat. Good Night!"

CHAPTER 6

LESSON 3

BILL RATIO TARGETS

Mark arrived at the office in the pouring rain, sopping wet. He had left his car to have the tires changed about a mile down the road and it started pouring halfway there. His folder with papers was limp and dripping. After getting him an old sweatshirt from the closet, no dry pants were available, but Graham had an old pair of coveralls covered with oil and paint that he used to work on his motorcycle in the back shop, they would have to do. Julia printed a new set of documents for him and tuned her laptop into the screen to project what Mark wanted.

Mark explained that while the $485,000 was the total payroll the firm needed to meet, the $381,000 was the direct cost of the time to generate maximum fees, and the difference, $104,000, was indirect labor covering everything else, administration, holidays, vacation time, the staff meetings, and so forth. He explained that on the operating statements his firm would prepare, the indirect time expense was tracked separately from the direct labor costs to better monitor performance.

"Today," he continued, "I want to work on the firm billing ratio a little more.

"First, think back to when we talked about the firm's revenue targets or chargeability, and that typical firms run from fifty percent—underperforming, to eighty percent—performing well but perhaps understaffed on the support side. With the numbers Julia calculated, you will be running at a potential of almost 81% (14,580 total hours, 11,767 available direct hours, Direct/Total = 80.7%). This is statistically too high. It will go down when you factor in some support staff. All revenue generators in firms like yours must earn revenue to support those employees that support them in non-billing ways."

"Could you walk through that on the white board?" Randy asked.

"Sure," and Mark picked up some markers and walked carefully to the board, not trusting the overalls to stay in place.

He wrote from his notes,

		Available Hours	Direct Hours
Julia	54%	2080	1123
Graham	75%	2080	1560
Cindy	90%	2120	1908
Adele	85%	2080	1768
Randy	85%	2080	1768
Clark	85%	2080	1768
Tara	90%	2080	1872
		14,580	11,767

"Dividing potential billing hours by total available hours you get 80.7%, say 81%," Mark summarized.

Turning from the board, Mark added "I want to interject some cautions. Every time period will be a little different. If you all broke your necks trying to hit the percentage next to your name every week it would not work. Too many things interfere with making a perfect score. We have already calculated in some of your indirect tasks, vacation, holidays, and the normal stuff, but what if you lost power for a day or had a major snowstorm where travel just couldn't happen? What if suddenly you lost some business and had to regroup? You can have cost overruns, or do-overs that are not compensating, so that's not fair to the individual who must put in the hours. Many things can upset hitting your target. Having a goal and monitoring to it is the important part, you know where you are and where you need to be. Another factor, at least for the balance of the year, is that you already have your fees locked in for the work in your backlog, unless you are just lucky, some of these fees are probably low or require more work than you can allocate billing time to. So, I suggest we reassess your bill ratio targets after we recalculate following the first of the year.

"The key is to measure toward a meaningful number—work to that. Be accountable to that while trying to maximize your earnings for the firm. In our firm, that target is ninety percent of your initial potential target number. We factor the difference into the bill rates we create. If we exceed this number as a firm, then it goes to bonus payments based on personal performance."

Mark reworked the firm target bill percentages on the white board.

Julia-Principal	54% – 50% x2080 =1040
Graham-Project Manager	75% – 65% x2080 = 1352
Cindy-Model Maker, part time Marketing	90% – 80% x2120 = 1696

(note changes when vacation increased to two weeks)

Adele- Electrical Engineer	85% – 75%x2080 = 1560
Randy – Mechanical Engineer	85% – 75%x2080 = 1560
Clark – Designer	85% – 75%x2080 = 1560
Tara – Intern	90% – 80%x2080 = 1664
Total	10,432

"This represents about a seventy-two percent time efficiency, adjusted to current circumstances of existing contracts. You've got five months left to the year, so if you calculate this time available into a five month block, you have a little less than 4400 hours to complete your backlog and any new work you bring in. You can each calculate your own number, and, Julia, it would be wise to sit down with Graham and estimate the work you have to see if there is capacity to complete it or to bring in new work without additional employees.

"All the formulas we are working on should be tested and compared to accurate time records. In the next meeting, we will examine your bill rates and then calculate the firm's potential annual revenue based on these bill time ratios."

Julia gave Mark a ride back to his car at the end of the session. "Sorry you got wet."

"Not a big deal, plus, it gives me a few minutes alone with you. What do you say to dinner Friday night, no business talk!"

"I'd like that, my treat, I owe you that, but you'll change your clothes by then, right?"

"Great, I'll book something expensive, and I'll dress up."

CHAPTER 7

LESSON 4

BILL RATES AND REVENUE TARGETS

The next Monday, Mark brought bagels and three flavors of cream cheese. He launched into his lecture before the first toaster load popped.

"This is an important day. The work you have done on time ratios and establishing your costs gives you the initial monitoring tools to track your performance. Until now, we haven't touched on a very key component to your success. Are you charging the right fees? It doesn't matter if your current project is a time bill or fixed fee project, it must be calculated at a sufficient fee if you are to be profitable."

"We pretty much copied what Bell Brothers used for hourly fees and raised them a little, but I have no idea if they are the right fees," Julia commented.

"Your fees should vary by discipline, by experience level, by responsibilities in the firm, importance to the clients, and some common sense, one being—will the client pay at this rate.

Let's play with some numbers," Mark Continued. We'll start with Graham—Graham's salary is $80,000. Not factoring in any benefits. Applying our base hour calculator of 2080 hours to that, he is paid $38.46 per hour. For everyone, this is how we get to our base rate to which we apply a multiplier to establish our bill rate. Sometimes, this is called a pricing multiplier. There is not one multiplier we can use to determine all bill rates. For most time-based businesses, the multiplier is highest for the lower paid members of the firm and a higher percentage of earnings usually come from these fees. The principal often is paid the most, but also has the lowest multiplier, usually. I will talk about why this works shortly.

"While there are no fixed rules, the multiplier will probably range between 2.0 to 6.0 times the pay rate. What we want to make sure we are doing is calculating bill rates that will result in acceptable fees for clients and at the same time allow for maximum revenue earnings for the firm when chargeability time targets are met. You monitor this and adjust over time. Let's work with your numbers. We'll use these to do some initial calculations and make some decisions."

Mark once again went to the white board and listed everyone's name. Next to each name, he put calculations to show multiplier rates and the resulting bill rate.

"This would be a typical starting place," Mark said.

Calculation of hourly payroll costs multiplied by a multiplier to create a bill rate (rounded) First Stab

Julia	$62.50	(x3)	$187
Graham	38.46	(x3.5)	$135
Cindy	23.07	(x4.5)	$105
Adele	33.65	(x 4.0)	$135

Randy	31.25 (x4.0) $125
Clark	26.44. (x3.5) $93
Tara	17.79 (x3.5) $62

Mark continued, "I'm going to give you my assessment on these numbers. You are a product development firm—your clients will sell the results of your labors at their standard mark-ups, generating revenues sometimes for many years on one completed product. This service is worth more than landscaping design for a building, for example, which is valuable but is probably not going to generate income and profits for the client. Therefore, you can afford to be a little on the high side of the bill rate spectrum. Again however, you do have some competition, and you are a newer firm, so you must use your gut a little and whatever knowledge you have about who is proposing against you to finalize proposals. This is an exercise you should go through periodically as part of your analysis as you are awarded or lose jobs. For the time being, based on my gut, I am going to make some suggestions.

"We will start with Tara. She has about one year on the job. She is helping all of you with tasks that keep you working on the more challenging aspects of applying your skills to the clients' project. This contributes to completing jobs on time, and at a high-quality level. Most of her hours go to revenue generation, but she does need some additional supervision as an intern in training.

"I think I would not go to the 5.0 multiple until next year but would use 4.5 as a multiplier. (17.79 X 4.5 = $80.00) this would help factor in the "you never know" lost time possibility. I think that is safe and profitable. Let's see what this means.

"If you keep her busy, she has 1664 hours available for revenue generation. If she achieves 100% billing efficiency on these hours, which we will discuss when we finish this exercise, she will bill $133,120."

"Wow" Tara said, "I'm incredibly valuable!" She sat smiling.

"Yes," Mark said, "as part of a team, that makes that possible. Do you think this is feasible for you?"

"If I have the work, I'm billing close to eight hours a day now."

"We will take Julia next, while she is still underpaying herself, she has an hourly rate of $62.50, if we applied a 4.5 multiplier to this, we would have a bill rate of $281. While product designers earn this rate and more, you are still in these early years of this business, so it may be a little high for generating adequate business at the level you are currently. Let's look at 2.5, or $156 - I think this is too low for a principal. Let's work with a multiplier of 3, $187.5, round up to $190. Julia is now at 50 percent revenue generation based on 2080 hours, that leaves 1040 hours at $190. This could generate $197,600 in billed revenue."

Julia just nodded, thinking.

"Next, Graham. While we've adjusted his time for his increased contribution to administration, its likely he will have a harder time hitting targets because as project manager he is the team's turn-to person for every situation that needs input. He is making valuable contributions to the clients even when it is not bill time. His fee should be the second highest in the organization. I think at 3.5 x $36.46 or $135 he is undervalued for his contribution. I am going to suggest just stabbing it at $175 (or a little less than a 5 multiplier). This fee will help offset time he is pulled away from revenue generation and the contribution he makes to clients that is not reflected in his time billing. Everything being perfect, Graham has 1352 available bill hours for a potential of $236,600.

"Adele and Randy, your rates are different, your pay is different based on your time with the firm. Your value to the client is the same, you are both senior engineers on projects. Your rates should be the same. At $135 and $125, these are bargains for the client. I feel safe saying you should be at the $150 an hour bill rate—this is about a 4.5 multiple based on Randy's pay.

Both Randy and Adele have a potential 1560 hours times the $150 rate = $234,000 each.

"Clark, you're less experienced, but it doesn't mean less talented, you supplement what Julia does in design and you feed work to the engineers and the model maker. However, from what I understand, you may be a slowdown point in production. I am not picking on you, but you and Julia must do design before engineers and model makers can do their work. I know you all work as a team, I am just being analytical. I think a lot is put on your shoulders, and a next move for the firm might be a second support designer to speed up design production, allowing engineering and others to have more backlog to hit their numbers."

"That would be great," Clark exclaimed. "I do feel like I'm holding others up at times."

Mark continued, "I think it is important to hit your number and push on work as quickly as possible to the design development disciplines. You also are newer to the firm, so you have to grow into a higher bill rate and salary, but I think I would peg you at $125—that's a potential revenue generator of $195,000 at your potential 1560 hours.

"Cindy, I left you for last."

"I noticed," she pretended to look hurt.

"Cindy is supporting each of you and each client by making your designs real in the form of models and prototypes. It's my understanding that this is not the case with some of your competitors, and I understand Cindy is really good."

Cindy smiled now.

"Modeling is one of your firm's signature services, and you win jobs because of it. There will probably come a time when you need more prototype modelers, and Cindy will have to help indoctrinate them into your operation. I am going to forget the multiples on this one, I think the service is in high demand, so I am suggesting $120. For the balance of this year, use this amount on new proposals and monitor the results. This represents a high 5+ times pay multiple, which may still be low. She easily has enough work to hit her hours, so $120 times 1664 hours represents $199.680. I would increase your multiple and bill rate when you have the rest of this year under your belt.

Let's total the results and talk about what to expect.

"You should each measure your week against the target hours we have calculated and discuss it in staff meetings. This will help you assess if you are at the right multiples and target hours, you can adjust over time." At the white board, Mark erased it clean and wrote the figures, underlining the total firm revenue potential.

Resulting Bill Rates

Julia	$190
Graham	$175
Cindy	$120
Adele	$150
Randy	$150

Clark	$125
Tara	$80

Possible Firm Revenue (all things being perfect)

Julia	197,600
Graham	218,400
Adele	234,000
Randy	234,000
Clark	208,000
Tara	115,200
Tonia	<u>199,680</u>
<u>Total</u>	<u>$1,406,880</u>

"Keep in mind, there are other influences that will interfere with the creation of a perfect time utilization record. It could be a reduced level of backlog, or a project that must be completed but has no billing time left. It could be any number of things, and your percentage will vary from period to period. The important thing is to strive for your allocated revenue target. During this initial period for you, it may be eighty percent or less, but over time, strive for that greater than ninety percent mark we discussed. We'll work on some important measurements for the firm in another lesson which will help keep track of where you are as a business."

Julia looked a little shocked. "Mark, that is considerably higher than our revenue for last year. I'm concerned that our clients won't accept these fees."

"Julia, use your gut, but try it on some contract proposals. If you win the commission, fine. If not, visit your prospect and ask if they would be willing to share where you came up short. If it is price, you will learn something, but remember, you are making much less than other firms of your type with the number of people you have. These tools are used by the more successful firms and have been effective for a long time."

Everyone agreed that trying was necessary.

CHAPTER 8

LESSON 5

PRICING JOBS

The Friday evening dinners became a regular thing. Mark paid over half the time, but Julia insisted they keep it fair, and occasionally she insisted on paying. One evening, Mark booked Pecola's. It had been Carl's favorite place, and the three of them, plus occasionally a date for Mark, had dined there frequently. Julia had not objected but was a bit curious. The owner greeted both by name and was genuinely pleased to see them again.

As they sat at their old favorite table, Mark asked, "Are you ready for this?" Mark swept his arm back, indicating he meant the restaurant.

"The restaurant? Oh yes, I miss Carl every day, but life has gone on, there's no reason we can't enjoy an old haunt, ah, no pun intended. Carl would be pleased."

"Julia, as you know, Carl was a dear friend of mine, and I respect him and his memory, but I wanted to dine here to include his memory in my next question."

Julia put on a quizzical look. "Go on."

"Are you ready to seriously date again?"

"Who did you have in mind?" she quipped.

Mark looked a little crestfallen at first but recovered, "Well, you could start with me."

Julia laughed.

"I have two tickets to *Hamilton* in New York in two weeks, are you up for a weekend in the Big Apple?"

"Were you desperate for a companion?" Julia wasn't going to give in easily.

"No, I'm trying to impress you, and I spent an arm and a leg to get these." Handing the tickets to Julia.

"Can you keep your limbs until we get back from New York?"

"Then you're in?"

"I'm in for the show, and I'm in to take our relationship to new levels by going slowly."

"Understood, I anticipated that we would I have a suite at the Thompson with two master bedrooms."

By December, the Monday meetings had dropped down to one a month. Mark congratulated all employees on adapting to the time keeping and tracking tools quickly.

"You are approaching the end of the year, so you'll have a fresh start with new year-long objectives as of January, but first, we have to make the best use of how the firm, and each of you, benefits from this work.

"We're going to establish measuring points that Julia and I can use in financial analysis to adjust as needed and to assure a more profitable operation. The more you understand and participate in this, the better for the firm and yourselves.

"These next steps will establish the report card of the performance of your firm and a tool to make adjustments.

"You recall in lesson two we discussed the firm's revenue generating ratio, which, collectively, is the

performance of each of you achieving degrees of your billing ratio targets. I want to take this a step further into a
very important tool Julia, and a future marketing person,
can use to ensure the growth of your backlog and business
by using the information to properly price jobs and to
monitor how efficiently they are executed. We'll call it the
direct profitability ratio, or some call it the Net Effective
Multiplier or simply NEM. Here is how it works. You now
all have an accounting weekly, monthly, and eventually
will have an annual number of your time as it is applied to
direct billing or job charge time, as well as a tracking of indirect time that goes to everything non-revenue
generating. This allows us to use the direct labor percentage as a multiplier and a tool for pricing. It becomes a
measure of your success and a tool for future success. As
an example, for November, you billed right around
$95,000. If you all hit your maximum targets, the total bill-
ing would be right around $117,000. As a result, you
achieved as a firm a percentage of eighty-one percent. This
is pretty impressive considering you haven't had a full year
at current bill rates and billing targets and you're still put-
ting a lot of time into old jobs that are not based on your
prior billing rates, plus, you have to factor in the Thanks-
giving holiday and any extra days off you've had this
month. You accomplished this by a lot of extra time over
the 40-hour work week, especially you, Julia. Next month
will be harder, especially since it will be basically a three-
week month. Therefore, monitoring these numbers based
on cumulative months is important. But let's make some
assumptions and double check again in February. Let's as-
sume you had a full year at the rates and targets we
established, and while you were still working off old jobs,
you had a cumulative ninety percent execution for the full
year. This is not unreasonable. Remember, this is a

40

percentage based on bill time, already adjusted to indirect time per person. It does not equate to the firm percentage that factors in all employee costs, including indirect employees—chargeability. Okay, bill potential $1,406,880. Achieved at 90% = $1,266,192."

Mark continued, "Your direct labor for the year, excluding benefits, is still $381,000. Recall the exercise where we broke your earnings into direct and indirect costs?

"To create the multiplier tool, you divide the revenue by the firm's total direct labor costs, the amount that went to generate the billing revenue or fees. 1,266,192 divided by 381,000 = 3.3 rounded. Checking monthly against annual performance and projected performance is critical to financial management of the firm.

"What it means is that for every dollar spent on direct labor, it generated $3.30 annually in revenue. Simply, this is the ratio of earned dollars for all direct labor costs, which you can now compare to a goal you set at the beginning of each year based on your time, multiple targets, and your billing percentage goal. This allows you to fine tune the targets and the firm over time and a lot more.

"My planning discussions with Julia have targeted 4.0 for next year, which will adjust bill rates and performance percentages, but have no fear that you will accomplish this simply by pricing your jobs better, reducing overruns, and having a balanced staff, and, yes, with some raises included." The team focused on just the last part. Mark added, "But raises must be factored to performance of your individual goals. Julia and I will address these early next year."

Julia had promised performance reviews after the year end financials and discussions of raises. She explained the additional hires would—should—help make the new 4.0 ratio happen.

Mark continued, "When you are quoting a job, you should each run a calculation of what you estimate your hours on your discipline for that job will be. Julia, you might adjust this based on historic information, but you eventually end up with a budget of hours to complete the proposed work. Now, calculate the direct labor cost for these hours and multiply by the target Net Effective Multiplier or NEM for your fee proposal before reimbursable expenses etc. are added in. If you calculate a job with a direct labor estimate of $40,000, your opening calculation based on next year's target NEM of 4.0 would be $160,000."

Julia commented "That's a lot better method than the dart board Graham and I have used, not literally, but sometimes it seemed that way. We used a best guess calculation, but we know it's hit or miss. Currently, we have two projects using time every week where we have no fee left to bill, and it hurts. With the NEM, we should be able to ace it every time."

"Almost every time," Mark added.

CHAPTER 9

LESSON 6

GROWING PAINS

Since lesson sessions were held at Julia's office, Julia hadn't been to Mark's office for a couple of months. It was a busy time with wrapping up the year end and projects with deadlines, plus, people missing a lot of time for holiday activities coupled with the flu taking its toll on the staff early in the new year, she felt like she had lost control of time.

She and Mark had a comfortable relationship, but to her it didn't seem to be going anywhere beyond comfortable dating, companionship, and an occasional overnight. Julia expected a ring and proposal at Christmas, but she got a necklace instead. It was a very nice necklace, but she couldn't help but be a little disappointed. On the other hand, her gift was not very romantic—she got Mark a hunting bow he had been making eyes at when they shopped at Drake's Sporting Goods. She didn't like hunting, but it was something he wanted. They had a pleasant Christmas dinner and evening all the same.

She was a little apprehensive entering Mark's building. It was a new year. Graham and Julia had recalculated hourly fees after everyone got a raise, reexamined their fee multipliers where it felt warranted, and were calculating all fees based on detailed hourly budgets and a 4.0 NEM target. They tweaked some proposals based on gut feeling for the client, competition, or the project itself. But they both felt all new work would be adequately profitable. They did lose two jobs to a competitor who lowballed them trying to keep IDD from getting the client—Intriguing Design and Development was now commonly referred to in the industry as IDD, and the team had spent one staff meeting designing a new logo. Julia knew the competitor couldn't make any money on their proposed fees, which eventually could benefit IDD.

The year-end had not been as good as Julia had hoped, but they made money, more than any other year. All employees met high percentages of their bill hour targets, but they were stuck with several older jobs that were not completed and had no billing time remaining. This was part of her current anxiety. The other complicating factor was that the backlog continued to grow through December and January, which made them late getting projects started, and she was making excuses to a couple of good clients that were being understanding, for now.

She felt she needed two new employees at least—one designer and one model shop assistant. Cindy was great but falling behind. She also had come to the conclusion that they could no longer go on growing and hope for profitability without a full time financial manager, and if she didn't get the office tasks and marketing time under control soon, it might be the end of her. She was still working sixty hours a week and was tired. Four new people meant new digs. The donut shop would exceed its maximum capacity with just two more people. Her real anxiety was money. How could she afford to do all this, but how could she afford not to?

Opening the door to the reception area, Julia was surprised when she was met with a young, beautiful receptionist who didn't know Julia from Eve. No coffee was offered. "Does Mr. Darden expect you?" was the greeting she received. Julia sat and waited.

When she entered Mark's office after a ten minute wait—the first time she'd ever waited—she noticed not one but two large bouquets of flowers on side tables by the windows and he was drinking from a new coffee mug (so coffee was available!) that read "Love You" on the side. Julia was relieved a moment later when she saw the other side, that added "not just because you're the boss."

She gave Mark a kiss and asked for coffee, "And by the way, who's the new model?" motioning her thumb back toward the entrance door.

Mark laughed. "That's Karla, daughter of my marketing director. We had a great year and gave great bonuses. Vern immediately requested to take her back-vacation time and took off for Italy, she'll be gone for six weeks. I had to act fast. Karla had some experience and it's a decent fit for a short time, I'll have her bring coffee, she should have offered."

Julia detailed her dilemma to Mark, and he listened politely until she finished.

"Growing pains are very real for businesses that become successful. It may be time for a real business loan or line of credit, but before we go there, let's add one more arrow to your financial quiver."

First hunting metaphor—he must be enjoying his new bow, Julia thought.

"First, let's look at what we call the overhead multiplier."

He continued, back in lecture mode, "All non-project, indirect costs, everything you didn't account for in your direct costs, is the starting point. Calculate this first for your existing costs, then for analysis, add in all your new costs for the two office positions and a new rent calculation. You now have your anticipated costs for this year including your new expenses. Include the indirect costs of your direct labor force.

"Now, take your new hires, calculate their bill rate the way we did all the others, and estimate their bill hour targets, being a little cautious since they must get up to speed. Calculate their indirect time at their salary rate and add it to indirect costs.

"To calculate the overhead multiplier, you divide the total of all these indirect costs, except bonuses when you get there, by your new direct labor costs. You can, and should, calculate this overhead multiplier for any period of time, but let's say a firm had revenue of $150,000 for January and direct labor costs of $85,000."

Mark did the math on his white board which was covered with numbers. He continued, "$150,000/$85,000 = 1.76. This is the resulting overhead multiplier. It means that for every dollar of direct labor, you spent an additional $1.76 in overhead costs. If you add the dollar of labor back into the overhead multiplier, you get your breakeven multiplier. In this case, $2.76. This is the point where you don't make money or lose money. You can compare this to your NEM number to calculate the firm's ability to make money.

"The lower the overhead multiplier the better, it will vary from month to month based on time charged to projects, but cumulatively it allows you to monitor costs and produced income. If this hypothetical firm had a NEM of 4.0, with the above 2.76 breakeven multiplier, it means the firm can generate profits of $1.24 for every dollar of direct labor.

"Julia, I'd suggest you run your current overhead and breakeven, then run it again with the added employees and new space and calculate expected revenue, and that will tell you if it's the right move or if there are tweaks to be made."

Julia felt she was getting the hang of managing by the numbers and felt less concerned. She was ready to dig into the numbers and make her decision based on the hard evidence it would produce.

As Mark walked Julia to the front office, he asked, "Like my bouquets?"

"Yes," Julia remarked, "admirers?"

"Sort of," Mark said. "The office had them delivered along with my mug after bonuses were given."

"Nice"

"Want one"

"Why don't you join me for dinner tonight? she asked loud enough for Karla to overhear, "and bring one along."

"Deal," Mark said, "see you around seven."

CHAPTER 10

RUNNING THE NUMBERS

Julia decided to work from home, even though she would be sacrificing some bill hours—this was important. She gathered all her financials, took them to the dining table, and started calculating.

She started with her new payroll

	NEW SALARY	CHARGEABILITY RATES (%)	DIRECT LABOR $	INDIRECT LABOR $
Julia	$136,500.	60	$81,900	$54,600
Graham	$85,000	75	$63,750	$21,250
Cindy	$56,000	90	$50,400	$5,600
Adele	$73,500	85	$62,475	$11,025
Randy	$68,500	85	$58,225	$10,275
Clark	$60,000	85	$51,000	$9,000
Tara	$40,000	90	$36,000	$4,000
TOTAL	$519,150		$403,750	$115,750
New Hire	$50,000.	90	$45,000	$5,000
New Hire	$50,000.	90	$45,000	$5,000
TOTALS	$619,150		$493,750	$125,750

So far so good, she thought. *Now I'll calculate what bill hours we will have at these rates.* She adjusted the typical fifty-two weeks, forty hours a week. She adjusted for vacations, sick days, holidays, and some required non-bill time. She didn't factor in a contingency, figuring she would do that in the financials instead.

She and Graham had reviewed and adjusted time pricing multiples after year end based on results of last year and their success at landing projects at the current rates. They decided on multiples person by person and adjusted where they though it appropriate.

	BILL HOUR TARGETS.	PAYROLL RATE HR ROUNDED	APPROXIMATE MULTIPLE	BILL RATE CURRENT
Julia	1128	66	3.0	$200
Graham	1410	41	4.5	$185
Cindy	1692	27	5.5	$150
Adele	1598	35	5.0	$165
Randy	1598	33	5.0	$165
Clark	1598	29	6.0	$165
Tara	1692	19	6.0	$115
New Hire	1764	22	4.5	$100
New Hire	1764	22	4.5	$100

REVENUE AT TARGET BILLING PERCENTAGES

	BILL RATE	GOAL HOURS	REVENUE
Julia	200	1128	$225,600
Graham	185	1410	$260,850
Cindy	150	1692	$253,800
Adele	165	1598	$263,670
Randy	165	1598	$263,670
Clark	165	1598	$263,670
Tara	115	1692	$194,580
New 1	100	1764	$176,400
New 2	100	<u>1765</u>	<u>$176,400</u>
TOTAL		12,481	$2,078,640

Here, Julia decided to factor in a contingency of ten percent. (207,864)

$1,870,776 (say, $1,870,000)

If the team exceeded the contingency target and achieved closer to the full chargeability target, then a bonus could be established.

Looking at the expense side was the next step. Julia started with a new rough operating budget.

Salaries	$619,150
Benefits	$123,830
Financial and office hire	$100,000
Benefits	$ 20,000
Rent	$ 30,000
New Rent ($5/SF x 5K)	$ 25,000

To these calculations, she added an overhead figure extrapolated from the prior years' operating statement.

Misc. Operating costs	$380,000
Total	$1,423,730

She decided this too needed a contingency of ten percent.

Contingency	$141,778.
Total	$1,565,508

She felt more comfortable with four new hires based on this work but was enjoying working with her numbers and wanted to get into the management benchmarks she had learned.

First checking the Net Effective Multiplier (NEM), this was her pricing tool and the measure of how effective they were in managing projects. It was crucial to hitting the revenue targets. She took the adjusted revenue budget of $1,870,000 and divided it by the new calculation for direct labor expense $493,750 for a 3.79 *4.0 to me*, she thought, without the contingency, it would be 4.2. Good execution could put them over 4.0. She was delighted, right on target. If they maintained landing jobs by using the multiplier, the NEM goal would be achieved.

Next, the overhead multiplier. She calculated indirect expenses using the indirect costs of the billing staff of $125,750 and added the indirect expenses from her new budget, including the new hires for finance and office— with some marketing help, she hoped. Benefit costs and new rent and a figure for all other operating costs pulled from last year's statement of $380,000 gave a total of $804,580.

She divided the indirect costs by direct labor costs $493,750 for a result of 1.63, arriving at her overhead multiplier. Mark had said the industry average was between 1.4 to 2.8. The number felt pretty good. She would be generating $1.63 in expenses for every direct labor dollar.

Based on the $1.63, adding back labor at $1.00, she had a breakeven of $2.63. She needed to generate more than $2.63 for every dollar spent on direct labor. Piece of cake! *I am getting cocky now*, she warned herself.

If they achieved the 4.0 NEM then deducting the 2.63 break even, the calculation allowed for $1.37 in profit for every dollar spent on direct labor. Multiplying the $1.37 times the direct labor of 493,750 generated a profit potential of $676,437, say, $675,000) more than her projected profit after contingency but she would be happy splitting the difference. She felt ecstatic.

She wanted to do one more calculation before ending the day and popping a cork to her future success. No, she would wait for Mark to arrive, get his input, and then pop the cork on a nice chardonnay.

She cranked up her laptop and connected to her desktop at work. She pulled up the Master Project List and began jotting down some numbers. When she was done, she had figured that they had three projects totaling 120 hours of work that didn't have any bill time left. It would be a priority to get these done and out of the way, and the time would reduce billed time. Other contracts totaled fourteen projects, and the hourly time budgets for these totaled 5,000 hours. Plus, she had twelve pending proposals. The 5000 hours represented about $875,000 in revenue, or forty-six percent of her projected revenue for the year, a very comfortable number. She felt that bringing in the contracts necessary to hit the numbers was quite do-able.

Time to prepare dinner.

She prepared sweet potatoes for roasting with rosemary and olive oil and set them aside, washed greens and wrapped them in a towel. The crème de la crème was her recipe for beef tenderloin rolled in fennel leaves, fresh basil, fresh oregano, and fresh thyme and roasted. It was so fragment you did not even have to eat it to enjoy it. She had given in and had a glass of chardonnay during preparation and decided a Côtes du Rhône would be better with the beef. She had both open when Mark arrived. He presented the bouquet, and Julia presented her financial study.

She poured him a glass of Chardonnay first, and he sat down to study her work. She sat across from him for five minutes just watching, and he didn't say a word, didn't ask a question, and showed no reaction. She decided to put some of the flowers in different vases and pour some more wine, now concerned with his reaction. It wasn't like him.

She had her back to him, and he finally said, "You're going to be a wealthy lady, I should marry you." She laughed, picked up the wine bottle to refill his glass and turned to find Mark on his knees holding a ring box out with two hands.

"Jules, will you marry me, please?"

"Before or after dinner?" she replied.

CHAPTER 11

PUTTING ALL THE TOOLS TO WORK

BASIC RULES WE EASILY FORGET IN THE EARLY YEARS

- Have a detailed time sheet for all employees and make it a cardinal rule to fill it in daily. Track direct and indirect time. Track Marketing time separately.

- Execute contracts that detail billing and payments with all clients. Use a business lawyer to help draft one that will protect you in all cases.

- Bill on a frequent and regular schedule. Do not let anything interfere with this schedule. Cash flow is the life blood of your business.

- Monitor all payment schedules. Request payment when it has not been received by the term of agreement.

- Stop work if someone goes thirty days overdue and let them know. Just be honest, you have a business to finance and employees to pay. The client will understand.

TIME AND CHARGEABILITY

SET CHARGEABILITY GOALS FOR EVERY DIRECT BILLING EMPLOYEE (INCLUDING PRINCIPALS)

- Start with 2080 hours.

- Deduct vacation time, sick time, individuals' indirect time responsibilities (estimated), then create an expectation chargeability goal for the year. Divide by weeks (excluding vacation) for weekly goal (I used to track this as a goal on my time sheet).

- Range 50% to 95% of available time. Principals are usually at a lower number.

COLLECT TIME SHEETS AT LEAST WEEKLY (some prefer daily)

EVERY EMPLOYEE SHOULD TRACK ALL TIME

- DIRECT (time generating revenue or posted to fixed fee projects)

- INDIRECT (all non-revenue generating time)

- Track indirect time for marketing and sales activity in its own category

- Track all time in 15-minute blocks with descriptions (this does not have to be complicated, if the task remains the same you simply draw an arrow through the time blocks).

MONITORING

- Monitor firm utilization or chargeability monthly (direct chargeable hours / total hours = utilization (chargeability)). Each direct employee has their own goal and should track their progress weekly and cumulatively for the year. Management should review with them periodically.

- Maintain a chargeability goal based on combined direct employee goals and indirect employee hours combined (60-75% factoring in all employee time - direct and indirect). The higher the percentage the better. This gives a picture of total firm chargeability with your mix of support and billing staff.

- Individual performance will vary but the expectation target over time is >90% of chargeability goal.

- Calculate direct and indirect time salary costs (excluding benefits and bonuses); monitor the percentage.

- If chargeability drops two months in a row, review all direct employee's actual chargeability to their goal. If there is a problem with individual employees, talk to them as to reasons why or what might be done. If it is more widespread, you might be low on work and need to act.

PRICING

CALCULATE A RAW HOURLY SALARY RATE FOR EVERY DIRECT EMPLOYEE (exclude benefits). (Salary divided by 2080)

- Use multiples of individual hourly rate to set rates appropriate to tasks, responsibilities, experience. (Typical 2.5-6.0.)
- When preparing quotations, create a budget of all-time tasks by individual and an expectation of total direct labor costs.

MONITORING

- Monitor multiples to gauge profitability and competitiveness
- Adjust for raises
- Track each project to the budget created, adjust budget procedure if you have multiple over or under budget projects. Suggestion: get everyone involved in budgeting their time and reviewing time of others—you will find ways to streamline production.

MONITOR BUSINESS OPERATIONS WITH KEY DATA BENCHMARKS

BENCHMARK ONE: NET EFFECTIVE MULTIPLIER (NEM)

(This measures your efficiency in executing project management, provides a pricing tool and a tool to monitor labor costs remaining on projects).

- Calculation: Divide earned fees for a period by direct labor costs for that period. (the NEM number represents an amount earned for every dollar spent on direct salaries).

- Target NEM range 2.8 to 5.5, set at beginning of each year, assess what is right for your operation, and that will provide the profits anticipated.

- Monitor monthly and cumulative months through the year.

- Monitor the NEM to achieve >90% of target NEM by project and total operations.

- Take action to adjust operations if NEM declines two months in a row (discounting December).

- Things to check with a declining NEM

  o Labor charged to projects that cannot be billed

  o Low bids, pricing too low

  o Work in process that is billable but is held until a future date

  o Inefficient execution of project tasks. Check employee time and performance.

- Use target NEM along with the time budgets to create estimates, proposals, and bids.

  o With a 4.0 NEM, you estimate it will take $47,000 in raw labor to complete the project. Bid calculation $47,000 X 4.0 = $188,000.

  o With a 4.0 NEM, you receive a $125,000 project, divide by four = $31,250 in raw labor costs, completing the work at this labor cost will maintain your 4.0 target.

OVERHEAD MULTIPLIER

- Calculate by taking all indirect expenses, include indirect time of direct employees and divide by direct labor
- Monitor monthly and year to date
- Range 1.4-2.8 (the lower the better)
- This monitoring benchmark will vary from month to month
- If the factor increases two months in a row (do not include December) your chargeability could be dropping, or overhead costs have increased.

STAFFING RATIO

We did not spend a lot of time on staff ratio in the text, but you can see how it affected Julia's overall profitability. There is a delicate balance between direct and indirect employees, finding the right balance for your business is something to pay attention to. You need enough indirect help to keep your business functioning efficiently and your direct employees devoting their time to revenue generation.

- Typically, time billing firms need a 3/1 ratio, direct to indirect employees or better to perform efficiently.

On the pages above, in chapter 11, the practical use of the tools presented in the text are summarized. This summary is available as a stand-alone document for your use.

If you found this book to be helpful, a review on Amazon or elsewhere would be most appreciated. It really helps writers to develop audience and sell their works.

Thank you for your time with Julia and Mark; they are very happy, and financially successful.

Mike